Ida Lee

The Bush Fire, and Other Verses

Ida Lee

The Bush Fire, and Other Verses

ISBN/EAN: 9783337256326

Printed in Europe, USA, Canada, Australia, Japan

Cover: Foto ©Thomas Meinert / pixelio.de

More available books at **www.hansebooks.com**

THE BUSH FIRE

AND OTHER VERSES

THE BUSH FIRE

AND OTHER VERSES

BY

IDA LEE

LONDON

SAMPSON LOW, MARSTON & COMPANY

Limited

St. Dunstan's House

FETTER LANE, FLEET STREET, E.C.

1897

LONDON :

PRINTED BY GILBERT AND RIVINGTON, LD.,

ST. JOHN'S HOUSE, CLERKENWELL ROAD, E.C.

TO MY

FATHER AND MOTHER

CONTENTS.

	PAGE
THE BUSH FIRE	1
BILL, THE GROOM	4
WHITE SEA HORSES	10
SUFFOLK	13
THE FISH-GIRL'S SONG	18
PHANTOMS OF THE SEA	20
THE WATER FROG	23
THE FOREST KING'S LAMENT	25
THE DROVER'S VISION	30
THE HOMESTEAD	34
THE BUSHMAN'S WOOING	44
THE VIOLET'S MESSAGE	49

viii   CONTENTS

                                          PAGE
TO A FAR DISTANT FRIEND   52

THE PROMISE   54

WHERE LILIES GROW   57

NATURE'S LESSONS   .   59

THE BUSH FIRE.

Stockman (*Loq.*).

Wake up, boy ! the grass is burning ;
See the glare across the hill !
Flames are nearing the " Flat Paddock,"
And the sheep are in there still.
Dark you say !   Yes, so I think it,
Tho' I see the field of corn ;
But the lights which flicker thro' it
Are not those we see at dawn.
Mount the Arab !   Take wet sacking !
Wet it must be, mind, not dry ;
We must save the master's cattle,
If we perish while we try.

Ride on faster, you are younger,
Tie your horse to yonder tree,
Break some overhanging branches,
One for you and one for me.

THE BUSH FIRE

Face the fire and do not shirk it,
Never mind the smoke and heat ;
Do not heed the dead wood cracking,
Or the sparks beneath your feet.
Beat and blind them, crush and kill them,
Till their blackened embers lie
Stark in ashes, and around you,
One by one in darkness die.

See the blaze is growing greater,
Now it runs with many a leap
To where stand the tall white gum trees,
In whose limbs the parrots sleep,—
Throws its fiery arms around them ;
Every bird in terror flies
From its home in grief forsaken,
Shrieking harsh unearthly cries.
Will the wind not turn to Westward,
Or those great black clouds drop rain ?
There was thunder ! no, I doubt it,
But do listen once again.

Now I hear the poor sheep bleating,
How they gaze from out the gloom,

THE BUSH FIRE

Like the stake-bound men we read of
Who have died the martyr's doom.
Just this moment they were rushing
Thro' the scrub down to the plain,
Parch'd and weary.   Now returning,
They seek refuge here again.

.   .   .   .   .

It was thunder !   It is raining,
For the cinders, hot and red,
Hiss, as cool drops fall upon them
Through the branches overhead.

Sweetly blows the yellow wattle
'Cross the road and up the lane,
But to me the scent is sweetest
Of the damp and moist'ning rain.
How it plays upon the firewood,
With a pattering ceaseless sound,
Like some grand and glorious music
Sent to soothe the saddened ground.
Take my arm, boy !   I feel blinded !
'Tis with joy from such a sight.
Lead me home.   I will thank God there
For His love to me to-night.

" The Bush Fire" *appeared in* *" The Sydney Mail"* (*Christmas Number*), *December* 19*th,* 1896.

BILL, THE GROOM.

THE lights burn in the stable, and I stand in the yard,
Yet thro' the open window I hear him breathing hard ;
They watch the bed in silence where Bill the groom
lies still,
For Bill the groom is surely fast going down the hill.
'Twas only yestereven, he made a solemn vow
To catch and ride the chestnut ; she stands outside there
now,
While he lies crushed and helpless upon a bed of pain ;
He will not see the sunset behind " The Ridge " again.
The chestnut's free and easy, a trifle too thin-skinned,
I know she isn't faultless, though sound in limb and
wind ;
But I thought she'd give no trouble, for Bill said he
could ride,—
Australian-born he was not, he came from t'other side.

4

BILL, THE GROOM

The young ones like to tell us the way they do things
    there,
And tho' I always listen (you know that's only fair),
I wonder what would happen on those great spread-out
    plains,
If when I rode " The Nigger," I let hang loose his reins.

When Bill first said he'd ride her, I think I did say
    " no,"
We told him all about her, the way that she would go,
That she had bucked and thrown us whene'er she'd got
    the chance.
Bill leaped the fence and caught her, she led him such a
    dance !
He put the saddle on her, it was not nearly tight,
I ran across and fixed it,—and he rode out of sight.
The hay-shed hid them from me, I watched them 'long
    the fence,
The mare then walked so quietly, I thought she'd learnt
    some sense ;
I know he'd got his stirrups, and held the reins quite
    straight,
And sat his saddle firmly as he went out the gate.

BILL, THE GROOM

I went and fed his horses, and forked their straw all
round,
Then something seemed to whisper that Bill was on the
ground ;
I thought I heard him calling, but when I raised his
head
His face was white and fainting, he looked to me quite
dead.
I don't know how it happened ; but there ! my eyes
grow dim,
I helped him mount the chestnut,—and she dealt his
death to him.

We brought him in and laid him upon his bed to rest,
And night and day we've waited, just hoping for the
best,
And done our utmost for him—the family are away,—
The doctor says he cannot see out another day ;
Tho' living's mostly trouble, my life I'm sure I'd give,
If I could bring back yesterday, and let poor Billy live.
He's waking now, they tell me, but not for long, poor
lad,
If he but had his mother, 'twould make his end less sad.

6

BILL, THE GROOM

For years they have been parted, yet strange enough it
seems,

Last night she came in spirit to calm his troubled
dreams.

They say she is in England, across the ocean blue :

I know she here was watching her boy the long night
through.

Don't say it all was fancy! I'm not a bushman
raw ;

Bill saw her when she entered, first in the open door,

He followed every footstep until she reached his bed,

And caught her hand and held it, as she stroked his tired
head.

And when she rose to leave us, the light, a narrow
streak,

Crept underneath the windows, and tears stole down her
cheek ;

Her face was drooping lowly, it looked so pained and
sad,

As once her glances rested upon the sleeping lad.

.   .   .   .   .   .

He asks about his horses, and wants to bid good-bye

To " Colonel " and to " Captain," to " Mill " and
" Marjorie,"

7

And even to the chestnut ! he says it was his fault,

She only bucked just once or twice, and when she
seemed to halt,

He pulled against the bridle, then up she reared in air

And fell right over on him—he lay beneath her there.

Come, wheel his bed among them and turn them in their
stalls,

'Tis hard if he can't see them before his strength quite
falls.

They seem to know he's going—they lick his outstretched
hand,

And as he speaks they whinny, the sight is really
grand !

But when he sees the chestnut (for in the door she
stood),

I never thought a youngster could be one half as good,

He pats her, and he pets her, and strokes her bright red
mane ;

The beast I'm sure is sorry she's caused him all this
pain

(I do believe I'm crying, tho' Bill wears such a smile,

He hardly could be wicked with a face so free from
guile).

BILL, THE GROOM

And there, among the horses, he said he heard a call,

Tho' everyone kept silent and solemn thro' it all.

His voice once broke the stillness, " That's not the stable
   bell ?

The angels call me, mother ! "—I caught him as he fell ;

We did not try to raise him ; I saw it was no use ;

The horses they were standing, with halters swinging
   loose,

To watch our every movement : we took his bed inside,

And now I know they're grieving because poor Bill has
   died.

WHITE SEA HORSES.

GLAD sea horses ! Sad sea horses !
  Rear the head, and toss the mane,
Spread out wide in bands together,
  Face the boundless deep again !
Grand white horses ! Stand, white horses !
  Just one moment calm and still,
In the bright and sparkling sunshine !
  None would dream your wrath would kill.

Great sea horses ! Stately horses !
  When you gallop still be kind :
Where is strength to curb your fury,
  Where are reins your mouths to bind ?
Urging onward, surging onward,
  Wild your onset, fierce and free !
Proudly rides a ship to battle
  O'er the line 'twixt sky and sea.

WHITE SEA HORSES

Wait, white horses ! Bait, white horses !
  While you don those trappings new ;
Now your noble chests are wrapt in
  Sumptuous folds of green-fringed blue.
Tall white horses ! Small white horses !
  Can it be in peace or war,
Thus you madly race the ocean
  Till you reach the sand-strewn bar ?

Champing horses ! Ramping horses !
  Mid the roaring, mid the noise,
Ere your fetlocks churn the billows,
  Proudly they uplifted poise.
Darting horses ! Parting horses !
  They have broken loose away,
Flinging far behind their traces,
  As they plunge among the spray !

Racing horses ! Pacing horses !
  When you speed with foam-shod feet,
Does, unseen, some ghost or spirit
  Prick your flanks with spurrings fleet ?

White Sea Horses

Vain sea horses! Strain, sea horses,
  With the sinews you possess,
Dashing high, above the waters,
  Heads which never knew distress!

Fighting horses! Biting horses!
  Open mouths and nostrils wide,
Arching necks and tangled forelocks,
  Snapping jaws on either side.
Fierce wild horses! Pierce wild horses!
  As the ship doth glide along,
They have struck athwart the bulwarks
  Blow on blow, dealt loud and strong.

Mad white horses! Bad white horses!
  Has the vessel spoilt your chase?
How you turn aside to lash it,
  In a passionate embrace!
Splashing horses! Crashing horses!
  Soon you frolic left and right,
Angels guard storm-beaten sailors
  Who encounter you to-night!

SUFFOLK.

AN EVENING IN AUTUMN.

GRAY shadows speed the fading day,
And creeping mists assert their sway ;
They rise arrayed in varied hue,
From sober black to faintest blue,
As smoke mounts o'er a slumbering fire,
Or lingers round some funeral pyre.
Across the fields and in the wood,
Where pheasant nestles o'er her brood,
No sound is heard ; the lifeless trees
Scarce move their branches in the breeze,
And fallen leaves lie curled and damp
Where glow-worm shows his tiny lamp.
Soon too with day the shadowed light
Will folded sleep, in arms of night.
Upon the marsh and up the hill
Wild rabbits scamper with a will.

SUFFOLK

The crimson sun so warm and red
Now sunken lies, in regal bed,
And tinted clouds float gently by,
Like rose-leaves o'er a painted sky.
The bending river wends its way,
Through meadows green where oxen stray ;
It stretches out its lengthy arm,
Which twists and turns past heath and farm.
Here, wild fowl often make their nest,
And plover, too, with golden crest,
From off its banks will fly or run
Amid the reeds at setting sun.
The village wrapt in sweet content
Reviews, ere night, the day well spent ;
And cotters lean without their door
To talk with friends the season o'er.
Beyond the sward, smooth lies the beach
Whence mighty waters onward reach,
And to the shore still rippling send
Sweet murmurings that do not end.
So softly do the wavelets move,
They seem to breathe but words of love
As if they feared or trembled, lest
They hurt one shell upon its breast ;

Or cast one pebble on the sand,
Lest it should know their strength of hand.
Thus fades the day before my sight
While nature waits the coming night.

MORNING.

DARK broke the daylight, cold and gray,
And sea-birds flecked the foaming spray,
Above the deep.   The waves now dashed,
And rolling huge, so heavily lashed
Their watery fleece against the strand.
But yesterday, with loving hand,
They laved its face with warm caress,
And softly on its cheek did press.
The glowing sun, which blessed that day,
Now frowning clouds hid far away.
No tinted rays could burst the veil,
Which falling thick in showers of hail,
And stinging sleet, that blew so fierce,
The smallest floweret seemed to pierce ;
And tossed aside the golden sheaf,
Or cut like steel each tiny leaf.

SUFFOLK

The breeze arose, but not to jest,
Or soothe those fears which breathe unrest ;
It sprang up strong—not lightly gay—
Nor deigned with one rose-leaf to play ;
But rushing madly to the wood,
Uprooted trees as there they stood,
Then threw them down among the gorse,
And crushed the ferns with cruel force.
When, whistling by the sea-girt dale,
It caused the fisherwife to pale ;
And made the worn-out rafters quake,
The sleepers suddenly awake.
The busy smacksmen set their sail,
And trim their boats to ride the gale ;
While aged seamen creep in sight
To glean the dangers of the night.
They long to join the gallant band,
Though wan of face and weak of hand,
And gaze upon the angry sea,
Which stirs the fading memory
To bring some peril past to each,
A lesson new, their age to teach,
When walking back to humble cot,
Each ache and ailment is forgot.

SUFFOLK

And in their homes the threadbare tale
Of wreck and rescue will not fail
The hours to enliven thro' the day,
And chase aside the shadows gray,
Which, round their lives' uncertain sea,
Now deepen where the warnings be
Of one last voyage which must be made
Ere sailings be for ever stayed.

NOON.

At noon's sweet hour came peace once more,
Wide open Nature laid her store
Of fragrant flowers—the birds sang gay,
To blot the sins of dawn away.
The sea herself, though foaming still,
Acknowledged then a stronger will,
Altho' at night the mourner's tear
Fell thick and fast.   Yet ever here
Tears dew the sorrow-stricken eyes,
While grief sits by to foster sighs.
Men only learn in Heaven above
The wisdom of our Father's love.

THE FISH-GIRL'S SONG.

CLANG ! Clang ! Clang !
I set my basket down ;
The bells hang high in the belfry tower,
And tell the folk 'tis the evening hour,
    Through in and out the town.

Clang ! Clang ! Clang !
O hush my wooden shoon !
When gently I swing the sacred door,
And kneel me down on the marble floor
    To beg a heavenly boon.

Clang ! Clang ! Clang !
Be silent, wooden shoon ;
And cease your noise while I say my prayers,
When vespers soar through the winding stairs,
    Up to the lonely moon.

18

THE FISH-GIRL'S SONG

Clang! Clang! Clang!
Good things all end too soon ;
I bow the knee as I say good-bye,
To holy place, with its spire on high :
Such restless wooden shoon !

Clang! Clang! Clang!
Work, morning, night and noon ;
For daily bread, and for nightly rest !
My heart is cheered and my soul is blest,
Ring out, O wooden shoon !

PHANTOMS OF THE SEA.

BLACK phantoms gather o'er the sea,
And move in groups mysteriously ;
With shears in hand they watching wait.
The night grows old ; the hour is late ;
The ocean foams with angry glee,
Its waters roll tempestuously,
And dash the white salt-spangled spray
Against the rocks, in rudest play.

The glimmering light around, below,
A sad wan face there fain would show ;
But darkness claims the night's last hour,
Enchaining it with mystic power.
In rugged outlines where they stand,
Tall, spectral cliffs shut out the land,
And shelter lend those forms who creep
On evil wings above the deep.

PHANTOMS OF THE SEA

All noiselessly, with one consent,
Their work but on one object bent,
They carry out a sovereign will,
And never rest, and ne'er are still.
They look like beings who frequent
A nether world—their time is spent
In weaving sorrow, grief, and pain
For those who sail the boundless main.

Quite unaware, from out the night,
A ship glides forth so tall and white
Amid the darkness.   Straightway she
Steers headlong to Eternity.
The vessel bears across the deep
A freight, who all unconscious sleep.
Gray gloom hath topped each frowning height
Which rising phantoms hide from sight ;
With outstretched hands in air they loom,
The ship to beckon to its doom.
But no, not yet ; 'tis not to be ;
Thou'rt cheated !   Look, thou angry sea !
Above the heights, there doth appear
A form, upholding high a spear

Of sparkling light ! It is the morn !
The night is dead ! The day is born !
" Begone ! " she cries, her hand she rears ;
" Bend low your heads, let fall your shears !
Away, you evil-meaning bands !
Aye ! Hide your faces in your hands.
Together link yourselves and flee,
And leave the brave in peace with me."

The ship is stayed. The helm they turn,
While sailors' hearts within them burn
To see the rocks, the seething foam,
The whirlpool eddying round its home,
And giant cliffs so near at hand.
A treacherous path those spirits planned,
To lead them onward to their doom.
There soon they must have found a tomb,
Had not the morning's early light
Reclaimed them from the clutch of night.

THE WATER FROG.

I WANDER far by bank and stream,
   Then paddle back thro' wave and foam,
Cross pebble stones, where waters leap ;
   A froth-clad doorway hides my home.
'Neath fern leaves' shade I gently dream,
   While circling weeds around me throng ;
The restless waters softly flow,
   Their babbling sounds like some sweet song.

When stronger grows the northern breeze,
   The driven stream with noisy roar,
Blown foremost by the boisterous wind,
   Bursts headlong thro' my shivered door.
A twisted twig I hop or climb,
   'Tis maddening pace at times we ride ;
First, twirling gaily round in air,
   Then smoothly on the waters glide.

23

THE WATER FROG

Great frowning rocks above look down :
　　With scornful glance they watch my glee,
Aloud I croak, and broadly smile,
　　What matter if they angry be ?
Our fleeting life is far too short,
　　Tho' merry as it well can be ;
The good, together with the bad,
　　Can sweeten still this world for me.

And when I reach my cosy home,
　　The bubbling waters shout " Hurrah,"
And hurrying onward, tell the tale
　　To other streams both near and far ;
How I have braved the tempest's din.
　　And now beneath the lofty pine,
While angry thunders make reply,
　　In sweet contentment I recline.

THE FOREST KING'S LAMENT.

Where linger the people I once called my own ?
In depths of the forest I stand here alone ;
Where waits my beloved one, my queen and my bride ?
'Twas seldom she wandered thus far from my side.
I hear not, I see not the world where they live ;
No day-dream reveals it, or comfort will give
To passionate longing ; hope dies in the heart
Of man when he dwells from his fellows apart.
With weary complaining I question again ;
'Mid rivers and mountains I hear a refrain
From cliff to the valley seem clearly to ring—
" Alone in thy kingdom where once thou wert king ! "

From over wide seas the white chieftains had come
To rest in our mountains and claim our dear home ;

The Forest King's Lament

'Twas morn in the vale when we rose up to fight,
'Twas darker than darkness, that fell ere the night.
Our farewells were short, as thro' thicket we sprang,
All armed with sharp spears and the curved boomerang ;
My people loud shouted their battle-cry old,
A quick answer came, by the bullet soon told !
I prayed as I fell, " May I speedily die
With those who, around me, now silently lie
Like reeds in a tempest, struck low by the rain,
Who never to life will awaken again ! "

I dragged myself back, yet scarce knew it was day,
Or if any escaped from the heat of the fray ;
No voice there I heard, not a sigh, not a sound,
As fainting, I lay on the grass-trodden ground.
But morning brought life, and the noonday gave strength,
The day slowly passed, and with evening at length
(Kind Nature had nourished my famishing frame)
I found I could rise, though enfeebled and lame.
Though why should I value that newly found breath ?
For bitter is life to me, sweeter is death,
And if I felt sure I should find them at last,
With joy would I join those true friends of the past.

THE FOREST KING'S LAMENT

I've sought the deep hollows, the gorge, and ravine,
From mallee to plain not a creature is seen.
White chieftains have journeyed and left me to rest,
They scour all the country from east to the west.
Alone in my camp, now, when fadeth the day,
I sit in the firelight the lizard to flay ;
Tho' nights are as fine as were those we could choose
To dance the corroboree, feast or carouse
Around the bush fire piled with myall and pine,
And box, red and white, or the cedar-wood fine !
Once danced we the war-dance from dark till the dawn,
And stayed not to rest until sunlight was born.

Warm sunshine still plays among myriad leaves,
Where silver-like thread the tarantula weaves ;
I see thro' the green the bright web he hath spun,
And kingfishers dazzling the light of the sun ;
From nests in the banks quick they flash in and out.
While jackass sits laughing with comical shout
'Mid branches o'erhead, wearing plumage of brown,
The river beneath floweth steadily down.
Thus murmuring, the ripples bring tears to my eye,
They sound like the tones of my loved one's reply ;

The Forest King's Lament

I turn right away, just to stifle the pain
Of knowing she never will hear them again.

Alone on the marshes the water-hens float,
With cresses and rushes surrounding their throat,
They pluck at the circles of mud-coloured slime,
Which harden and bake in the summer's sweet time.
If water be scarce, or if river run dry,
There sandpiper, too, on occasion will hie,
And heron or pelican often be seen,
Food patiently seeking in silence serene.
At times I do wonder if haply they know
What power has arisen my sway to o'erthrow ?—
What memories they stir !   When they rise on the wing
I dream of the days when I reigned here as king.

The wattle's scent mingles with that of the briar,
Where tower the white gum trees in noble attire :
In days when we hunted the emu abreast,
'Twas under their shade we would lie down and rest,
Till curlew at evening poured wail upon wail
That circled the forest and crept thro' the vale,

THE FOREST KING'S LAMENT

Then, meeting the echoes amid the wide plain,
Would rise there and fall there, and circle again.
Do yearnings increasing disturb the strong breeze,
That moans in the brushwood and grieves in the trees ?
Its sob overcomes me, no more can I sing,
But bend low in anguish where once I stood king !

THE DROVER'S VISION.

THE drover's camp one evening in hushful calm lay still,
Its fitful flickering firelight made bright the western hill ;
The bronzed and bearded drover had stretched himself
    to rest,
In childlike peaceful slumber, his arms across his breast.
His saddle formed a pillow, the thick, coarse grass his
    bed,
While mounting sparks were casting a halo round his
    head.

Then sweetest dreams came pouring to charm the weary
    brain,
He saw his mob of cattle outspread upon the plain ;
But curling whip lay silent, and watchful dog slept sound,
As deeper grew the stillness which held its sway around :
Thro' forest paths an angel had sped with hurried haste,
The twining leaves he forced apart until he reached the
    waste.

THE DROVER'S VISION

Past many growing townships, o'er tracks of sun-dried
    plain,
And rocky hills and rivers, he brought his tale of pain.
Long shadows rose to meet him ; in groups they
    gathered round,
While trees unbent and listened in reverence o'er the
    ground,
Where hallowed steps had fallen, where an angel late had
    trod,
Whose holy feet with pity, and love, and faith were shod.

The drover heard those footsteps ; he felt an icy breath,
And, turning round in greeting, beheld the face of Death,
A vision bending o'er him, and holding, gently down,
A tiny suffering infant whose life had well-nigh flown.
It raised its fragile body, and softly turned to rest
Beside him, closely nestling against his massive breast.

And, as the shadows parted, the small wan features
    smiled
Upon him, oh ! so sweetly, and he saw it was his child.
A moment more, it left him, and thro' the dimness fled
Back to the Angel vision, with tiny hands outspread.

The Drover's Vision

The white-robed arms enfold it, and glances sweet and
  rare
Fall on the stricken drover, who lies in darkness there.

When morning breaks, the sunshine streams over a
  moving throng
Of cattle pressing onward, while breezes bear along
The sound of parrots' chattering ; and sweet toned bell-
  birds sing,
Like chimes on a Sabbath morning, their notes through
  the bushland ring,
And tall trees wave their branches athwart the rosy
  light,
Forgetting in their pleasure, the sorrow of the night.

The drover's world is darkened, his heart is wrung with
  pain,
As gazing o'er the hill-side where his ash-strewn camp
  had lain,
He thinks of the vanished spirit and heavily droops his
  head,
While sadness sits in his saddle—he knows his child is
  dead.

The Drover's Vision

He prays with fervent pleadings that his babe may stay
its flight

In God's own Heavenly Kingdom—His home of love and
light.

THE HOMESTEAD.

THERE stands the homestead ; white amid the trees
So lowly set, where stirs a faint warm breeze.
Across the sward the thronging cattle pass,
Their colours blurred, as, in one moving mass,
Loosed from the yard, the panting creatures seek
Their restful pastures by the flowing creek.
Yet sunlight lingers in the crimson leaves,
And, where it touches, softer beauty weaves.
It plays around the open entrance-door,
And casts its glowing radiance on the floor.
See on each drooping flower whose heavy head
Bows the tired stalk, the dying sunbeams shed
A faded splendour, lending deeper grace
To all those colours which their rays embrace.
All through the day the busy droning bee
Has music made by every flowering tree,

34

The Homestead

And sipped the goodness from the blossom sweet,

Which bursting full bloomed in refulgent heat.

Now where the shaded corner screens the hive,

The laden workers one by one arrive,

With merry hum and din, the tiny throng

Fill the cool garden with their evensong.

Long slanting shadows creep from out the shade,

And clouds above accumulate and fade.

In one short breath, like foam upon the sea,

When rising winds the ocean bubbles free,

They shape themselves and vanish into space,

And others quickly follow in their place.

The heated day departs, yet gentle night,

Though venturing nearer, veils her face from sight,

Patient awaiting that belovèd hour

When like a queen, she rises, full of power,

To grasp the fallen sceptre of the day,

And calm her subjects, casting care away,

While freshening dewdrops cool the fevered land,

With gentle touch as of a mother's hand.

The great brown eagle hurries home to rest,

Amid the rugged mountains in the west:

Where yawning space asserts herself, between

The towering cliff, deep gorge and dark ravine,

THE HOMESTEAD

Where ferns and bracken grow, and interlace
Their beauteous fronds across the rock's stern face,
He lives a king, within a regal nest
The feathered monarch of the lonely west.
Above him sombre flocks of ibis fly,
On drooping wing, across the tinted sky,
And mar the beauty of its golden light
By their uneven lines and lengthened flight.
Upon the hillside, motionless and calm,
Like sentinels who shelter all from harm ;
The stalwart trees extend their branches white
And keep their silent watches through the night.

Behold, like glistening silver, quickly glide,
Yet farther off, the river's hurrying tide !
By sandy shores and widening banks it flows,
Till tranquil to the open sky it shows
A gleaming face, reflecting clear and true
Its answering gaze from out the deepening blue.
One spot alone defiles the sand's white breast,
Where some foul crawling snake a track imprest,
Recording by the broken mud-stained trail,
The linked contortions of its twisting tail.

THE HOMESTEAD

A solitary horse surmounts the steep,
Bringing its rider home to well-earned sleep.
The threatening troubles which his hand must stay,
The heavy toil, the worries of the day,
Are all forgotten, as upon the plain
He sees his homestead rise to view again.
A happy smile lights up his sunburnt face,
When on the breeze sweet voices he can trace,
Of those he loves who watch for him, and wait
To give him welcome at the open gate.

Upon the giant boulder's flattened stone,
Which bars the stream, in ages that have gone,
Where cool soft shade the river oak tree throws,
'Twas there the black man's spear uplifted rose,
And pierced the darting fish with matchless aim,
Then stooped his dusky arm his spoil to claim.
When summer evening too his world made bright,
And bathed the trees and flowers in crimson light,
The sunset tingeing red each leaf and bough,
And all the bush was beautiful as now,
Often he rose and wandered by the bank ;
Where grew the native thistles tall and rank,

The Homestead

With blithesome step, and sure unfaltering tread,
He traced a winding road ; about his head
The trailing creepers from the trees hung low,
And snow-white petals brushed his swarthy brow.
The hazy sun-spots danced and round him played,
While silken cobwebs shimmered through the shade.
And here and there the fragrant wattle leant
Across his path, as leisurely he went,
To where the open plains their limits kept,
Above the dense growth which the hillside swept.
Fleet would his dogs, with noisy bark, pursue
The bustard wild or startled kangaroo.
But time has changed ! The black man's race is run:
No more at even, when the dying sun
Is sinking to its rest, will he be seen
In that fair spot : the tufted rushes green
May conclaves form upon the wide expanse,
Still in the river-bend the fish may glance,
And waters chant their rhyming lullaby ;
But not for him. He never will descry
The painted plumage on the parrot's wing,
Nor listen where the woodland echoes ring,
With shouts of laughter from that peering bird
Who sits, convulsed, in attitude absurd,

THE HOMESTEAD

Amid the leaves which crown the shrunken limb
That slanting reaches to the waters' brim.
Advancing Time has turned another page,
And gives the land a new, a greater age.

Already too that young land, having past
Her childhood, stands to claim her place at last,
Already walks at her great Mother's side
Among the nations in majestic pride,
While Britain glances on that comely face
Whose every feature bears her stamp of race.
She guidance gave her through her infant days,
And lit her path with all ungrudging rays.
In early years the daughter learnt full well
To whom to trust her steps when darkness fell ;
While knowledge of the help and love she drew
From out her Mother's breast woke fondness true.
Yet still the daughter wore a listless air,
Dependent, and too young for thought or care,
Till came o'er foaming seas a rude alarm,
" Foes taunt thy Mother with uplifted arm ! "
The strength of her great parent she knew well
Could all unaided threats and foes repel !

But now she starts, stung by the hostile words
Of those who stand around with naked swords !
Upstirred, the ancient pride within her veins,
And courage quick, from caution snatched the
  reins.
She called her sons, the towns, the bushland
  through ;
Called them to arms ! Australians brave and true !
Resentment fierce, which could no longer hold
Itself in check, burned wild and uncontrolled,
That covert acts a noble queen distrest,
Or robbed fair England of her quiet rest.
Her sons obey, striplings and men full-grown
Prepare for war, and conflicts yet unknown.
With fearless mien, and flashing angry eye,
Each girds a soldier's sword upon his thigh.
A heightened blush o'erspreads his glowing cheek,
Erect he stands, though passing young to speak,
While from his brow he sweeps the kiss of sleep,
Which lingered there in languid rapture deep,
And filled his senses, letting him forget
The duty manhood made a sacred debt.
Quickly he sends across the billows wild
This message to the Mother from her child :

THE HOMESTEAD

" Think not that I can dwell in calm repose
While friends around thee waver, and rude foes
Goad thee to anger with coarse gibe and leer,
And flaunt before thine eyes the lifted spear.
From thee I rose : for thee I can but fall!
Thy need suffices for my battle-call."
The tones all quickly tell the sword gleams bare
Within the youthful hand uplifted there.
Her fond smile deepens as the Mother hears
Still further comfort which the ocean bears.
Her proudest glory is her children's love,
Who with their life-blood loyalty would prove.
When thro' the arid desert's sandy waste
The Royal standard presses in its haste
Around the Mother's flag, the foeman sees
Her daughter's banner floating in the breeze :
Those soldier-children in a southern clime
Sacred will hold that heritage sublime.
Let England's enemies remember well
The fortunes which the elder flag befell
On battle-fields, in troubled days of old,
Nor think her ancient spirit has waxed cold.
The past, the present, and the days to come,
Will show how sons of England guard their home !

THE HOMESTEAD

Great England! not thy sea-girt shore alone,
That stretches round the Queenly Sovereign's throne,
But all the widening sway, and boundless grace,
Of those vast countries which a world embrace,
Where dwell the sons of Britain. Ill betide
Who speaks against their country strong and wide!
Throughout the world one patriotic zeal
Binds the vast empire, as with links of steel,
To that sweet peaceful Isle we call our home.
Thither, from mountain top, or crested foam,
We turn our thoughts (as flowers turn to the sun),
And cherish high what there our fathers won.
If far away we watch the sunlight fade,
Beyond the range (where in past years, dismayed
The tired explorer stood, with weary brow,
And gazed across the mallee high and low),
We thrust the shadows back, and think the while
How men forget their fears to win her smile.
What danger will they face if to her name
'Twill add new lustre, or still wider fame!
Or if we stand within the city's pale
Where once rode armoured knights in coated mail,
Of those we think beneath its sacred dome,
So long since gone, who also called it home!

THE HOMESTEAD

And proud we feel in this brief passing hour,
That God with bounteous grace has given us power
To call it ours ! His strong far-reaching hand
Has kept a faithful watch above this land.

Light has departed ! In the western hills
Its place around the homestead darkness fills ;
Save in the windows, whence the smiling lamp
Outshines the gloom and cheers the distant camp,
Where with their flocks the drovers spend the night
In restful slumber until morning light.
One stage is finished ! stars gleam in the sky
As weary heads on pillowing saddles lie.
Around the men sweet dreams their cobwebs spin,
And soon shut out the day's unrestful din.
All through the air a new-born stillness grows
As sleep, around, a mystic thraldom throws :
Above, below, her soothing angels spread,
On beast, and bird, o'er things alive and dead,
Their blissful wings, while voices never cease
To chant in silvery tones a song of peace.

THE BUSHMAN'S WOOING.

" SHORT grows my leave," the bushman said,
  " My love I will avow ;
When I come back, the maid I'll wed,
  If she will hear me now."
So fair this maiden was, and bright,
  She'd suitors more than one,
But when the bushman rode in sight,
  She met him there alone.

She heard him speak of golden love,
  A blessing, deep and true,
Such love was theirs, he fain would prove
  If she would let him woo

44

THE BUSHMAN'S WOOING

And claim her there, when work was done.
　The maiden glanced adown ;
" Not thus," she said, " must I be won,"
　And smoothed her silken gown.

Then angry spake the man aloud ;
　He saw the hand, so small ;
While o'er his face there came a cloud,
　These words his lips let fall,
" A stockman may seem rough or rude,
　Yet all the while be bold,
'Tis not because the quartz is crude,
　It can't contain the gold.

" A bushman's life is wild and free,—
　That easy is to read,—
Don't live to learn just what you see,
　But take the will for deed.
Now all this time I know you meant,
　Not ' No ' to say, but ' Yes ! ' "
Then as he spake, the tall man bent
　His head, her hand to press.

The Bushman's Wooing

The maiden would not seem to see,
    But drew her hand aside,
"The man I love must courteous be,
    Ere I will be his bride.
You say the life is rough and wild,
    You think the man is bold ;
I still could wish the stone were filed
    That one might see the gold !

"To-morrow morn I'll hear your tale,
    And then, perhaps, I'll say
A word of comfort if you fail
    To win my love to-day.
My heart is not a paltry toy,
    Just worn upon the sleeve,
To give away to man or boy,
    Who barely asks my leave."

"At morn," he said, "I take the sheep
    Beyond the Queensland line ;
We start before you wake from sleep ;
    Just place your hand on mine,

THE BUSHMAN'S WOOING

And say, ' God bless you, Jim, to-night,
   And bring you safely back; '
I then can face the hottest fight
   Or meet the fiercest black."

All anger from his face had fled,
   His eyes with sweetness shone,
The maiden's cheek went white, then red,
   She stood as turned to stone.
Her lips they moved, as if to say
   Some words to reach his ear,
But minutes pass, and still they stay
   Pressed close as if with fear.

One moment more, and then he knelt
   Low at her feet to ask
The blessing sweet, for still he felt
   'Twould lighten all his task.
Her hand so small was stretched out there,
   And laid between his own,
And while he held it, white and fair,
   This maiden's pride had flown.

He felt her trembling fingers move,
  Yet low he humbly bent
Before her there to prove his love,
  The while she grew content.
And then she spoke, he scarce could hear,
  Her voice fell soft and sweet,
" Twas ' Yes ' I meant, I cannot bear
  To see you at my feet."

THE VIOLET'S MESSAGE.

ALL radiant was the garden with choice and precious
   flowers ;
Rare blossoms in their " houses " enwove resplendent
   bowers.
They were the rich man's treasures, he gave them every
   care,
And yet the dew of heaven could never reach them
   there.
They did not feel the raindrops, or sunshine warmly
   bright,
Nor winced beneath the dangers of a cold and frosty
   night.

The Violet's Message

For all were closely tended and spared from every
ill,

A gardener's hand had planted each flower with dainty
skill.

Now outside in the meadow, a modest violet grew,

And no one ever watched it, for no one ever knew ;

Still there it lived and flourished, and scent of flowerets
small

Was carried by the breezes across the high stone wall.

It reached the great man's window, was wafted thro' the
door,

And made the air seem fresher than ever it was before.

It reached the great man's heart, too, and whispered in
his ear,

To tell a loving message, in accents sweet and clear.

He saw once more his birthplace and childhood's happy
years ;

'Tis not a vision only, the brain both sees and hears.

There stands the old white cottage, long vanished from
his sight,

He feels the cool wind blowing across the fields at
night.

THE VIOLET'S MESSAGE

In waters of the streamlet that graced the woodland
scene,
He seemed to see reflected the man he might have been.
He sighed, " O gentle violet, so tender and so true !
Of all my rich collection, not one compares with you.
Your coming here has taught me, how I may walk each
day,
The paths where you are lovely in your sweet simple
way."

TO A FAR DISTANT FRIEND.

Eyes that are true,
Shadowed with blue,
Speak her sweet mind :
Out of her face,
Calm in its grace,
Looks the spirit behind.

Swift ocean tide,
Steep mountain side,
Stand now between :
Yet will my heart,
Sacred, apart,
Treasure days that have been.

To a Far Distant Friend

No sunlight plays

With the same rays

On her and me :

    Time's shortening wing

    Troubles may bring,

Clouding Life's restless sea.

    Still I will pray

    Her heavenward way

Thrice may be blest ;

    Angels to guide,

    Walk by her side,

Love her ever the best.

THE PROMISE.

WHERE are the angel-fingers
That traced the road I trod,
And pointed out so clearly
The heavenly way to God ?

Where are the noble faces,
The eyes, quick flashing light,
That warned me there was danger
Before it came in sight ?

Where are the cheerful voices
I knew in days of youth ?
Through every tone came ringing
A thrill of earnest truth.

THE PROMISE

Why did they tire and vanish,
  And leave me here alone,
To stumble on a pathway
  Beset with jagged stone?

I hear no sound to bless me,
  I see no hand to guide
My feet o'er thorny places,
  Or point where ways divide,

Though every sign-post tells me,
  That I have gone astray,
And arms for ever beckon,
  Yet, further lengths away.

My heart grows hot and weary,
  My soul is filled with care,
And thoughts around me thronging,
  Have quenched all wish for prayer.

I wail in keenest anguish,
  Must I sink beneath the sod,
On earth, not find my Father,
  In death, not reach my God?

THE PROMISE

The clouds above me open,
 And a glorious ray of light
Comes streaming out of darkness,
 A voice speaks thro' the night,

" You have a faithful promise,
 Escape for you is near,
When grows the tempter's presence
 Too great for you to bear.

" Arise and journey onward :
 A two-edged, flaming sword
Directs you to your Saviour,
 Through His Almighty Word."

WHERE LILIES GROW.

Where lilies grow ;
The dewdrops linger on the flowers,
The birds' sweet singing chimes the hours,
I love to sit there listening,
And watch the fish there glistening.
They glance and dart both in and out,
And turn themselves all round about,
    Where lilies grow.

Where lilies grow ;
A pace or two the violets sweet
Spread like a carpet 'neath my feet ;
The rushes tall in clusters stand ;
I reach and touch them with my hand ;
And yellow kingcups there unfold,
They circle like a band of gold
    Where lilies grow.

WHERE LILIES GROW

Where lilies grow ;
So calm, so still it is, and deep,
Around the edge green fringes peep,
Just up above the trailing weeds
Entwining, spread among the reeds,
Then hang them down along the pool,
Which lies beneath so calm and cool,
Where lilies grow.

NATURE'S LESSONS.

TELL me whether you have ridden
  Gallant steed a lengthy mile !
As he galloped, in your saddle
  Could you sit and calmly smile,
For you hardly felt the motion,
  Tho' his feet fell firm and strong,
Sending sparks in feathery flashes
  From the flint-strewn road along ?

Then did forests flit and vanish,
  Lofty trees like spectres pass ?
Looked the mountain in the distance
  Like some wavering shapeless mass ?

59

NATURE'S LESSONS

Could you only see distinctly
    Fine-cut ears and flowing mane,
While your fingers felt the snaffle
    Pulling doubly on the rein?

Have you ever watched the river,
    Bounding onward to the sea,
Have you heard the restless throbbing
    Of the waters' joyous glee,
From the upland to the valley
    Still so bravely battling on,
Turning not for gain, or pleasure,
    Till its goal is safely won?

Have you seen the kingly eagle,
    Rising, leave his nest on high,
Wings outstretched, eyes glancing sunward,
    As he cleaves the azure sky?
Quite as glorious as the river
    (For one hand has made the two),
Reared and dwelling near the heavens,
    Linking those blue heights with you.

NATURE'S LESSONS

When we sail across the ocean,
  Far from sight or reach of land,
Feel we then the vessel fighting
  White sea-horses in a band?
Fierce and wild they turn and double,
  Waves of water wildly moan,
Joining there they lash the bulwarks
  Till the ship will creak and groan.

Tho' the joy lay yet unconscious,
  Time in after days will bring,
Out of all such scenes, a token,
  Breathing of some better thing.
Our tired senses will awaken
  From their slumberings, fresh and strong,
While a holier spirit bids us,
  Love the right, and hate the wrong.

'Tis not thought of fame or fortune
  That rebounds within the mind,
Stifling every earthly passion,
  Opening eyes which long were blind.

NATURE'S LESSONS

There, revealed, lie noble secrets,
  What is greatest, noblest, best,
In our natures, then uprising,
  Make such scenes for ever blest.

THE END.